Outa the Rut:

Breaking Habits Before They Break You

Neil McK. Agnew Ph D

&

John L. Brown Ph D

Order this book online at www.trafford.com/09-0142
or email orders@trafford.com

Most Trafford titles are also available at major online book retailers.

Note for Librarians: A cataloguing record for this book is available from Library
and Archives Canada at www.collectionscanada.ca/amicus/index-e.html

Printed in Victoria, BC, Canada.

ISBN: 978-1-4269-0350-2
ISBN: 978-1-4269-0351-9

*We at Trafford believe that it is the responsibility of us all, as both individuals
and corporations, to make choices that are environmentally and socially sound.
You, in turn, are supporting this responsible conduct each time you purchase a
Trafford book, or make use of our publishing services. To find out how you are
helping, please visit www.trafford.com/responsiblepublishing.html*

*Our mission is to efficiently provide the world's finest, most comprehensive
book publishing service, enabling every author to experience success.
To find out how to publish your book, your way, and have it available
worldwide, visit us online at www.trafford.com*

Trafford Rev. 5/26/2009

 www.trafford.com

North America & international
toll-free: 1 888 232 4444 (USA & Canada)
phone: 250 383 6864 ♦ fax: 250 383 6804 ♦ email: info@trafford.com

The United Kingdom & Europe
phone: +44 (0)1865 487 395 ♦ local rate: 0845 230 9601
facsimile: +44 (0)1865 481 507 ♦ email: info.uk@trafford.com

10 9 8 7 6 5 4 3 2 1

"Everyone wants to change the world; but no one will change themselves."

— Leo Tolstoy

Contents

Preface

For over twenty years we've watched how people from all walks of life try to break old habits – some succeeded, many failed.

Those who succeeded typically followed the steps outlined in the following pages.

Not only did they climb out of their ruts but they discovered better futures.

Before escaping they admitted wasting hours, weeks, years mindlessly goofing off but getting no long term satisfaction from this massive investment. Then they smartened up, made wiser investments of their non-renewable and most precious resource – *their time*. For example one started browsing quality stuff (moving from e-bay to Wikipedia and finally discovering ted.com), then set up her own web site focusing on possible futures. Now she's learning interesting stuff, meeting fascinating people - "It's almost as good as sex."

We're talking about "flow". **Flow** is a psychological state in which a person is fully immersed in what they're doing, a high energy, focused and productive condition. If you're interested in learning more Google "Mihaly Csikszentmihalyi " the father of flow.

Note: The suggestions in this book are not designed to treat clinical conditions. Those suffering from debilitating psychological or behavioral disturbances are advised to seek professional help.

Acknowledgements: Over the years the authors have benefited from the collaboration of others. In particular Lucie Cantrell and Bill Scott at York University helped develop SCAMP, a Self-change and Management Program, on which many of the ideas in this book are based and in which hundreds of people participated. However Lucie and Bill are not responsible for any of our idiosyncratic applications.

Why not give it a try? Why not run your own self-change and management program. We've found that if you work it works.

Chapter 1: Just Blew Another Resolution

"I'm a walking skin full of failed resolutions"

Remember those pearls of wisdom that sound great? Such as: *"Today is the first day of the rest of your life."* You paste it on the bathroom mirror … e-mail it to a friend … resolve to smarten up!

What happens?

Life happens. It pushes the frail intention aside. Things drift back to 'normal.'

Why? It isn't that you don't know better. Obviously insight is not enough.

But some people actually do change. Besides hating them for their smug success what can we learn from them? What's their secret?

As we'll discover throughout this small book it's not all that complicated.

Smart people solve tough problems by thinking outside *their box.*

How do they escape out of their box, outa their rut?

Figure 1-1

Like all escape artists they use tools. For instance by using analogies and metaphors they slide outside their habits and explore and find new paths.

Einstein did it —'imagine you're on a train traveling at the speed of light.' He called his explorations *thought experiments.* Some of them actually worked, actually worked wonders!

In subsequent chapters we present simple thought experiments that help break bad habits before they break you.

You don't have to ride a train traveling at the speed of light – you can choose your own mode of transportation, your own speed, and your own destinations.

Figure 1-2

Chapter 2: Who's the Boss?

Who's the boss of your life?

Who's driving your train?

Thought experiment #1: When you think *inside-the-box* the obvious answer is: "I'm the boss" – I'm steering my train."

The popular analogy goes like this.

It's *as if* there's a tiny 'you' sitting on top of your brain, operating the controls, giving orders: "Get up… brush your teeth… drop off the kids at school … go to work… finish report… go to lunch… attend 2 o-clock meeting, … then happy hour, etc., … etc., … watch the 11 o-clock news, brush your teeth, get into bed, …'sorry, I've got a head ache'… go to sleep."

Poets glorify this analogy of a little you operating the controls: "I am the master of my fate, I am the captain of my soul."

Philosophers call it "free will."

We'll call the little boss inside your head '**Tiny**'.

Figure 2-1

Most of the time you believe Tiny's running the show - you believe in free will. Your family believes it, your friends believe it, your boss believes it, the tax department believes it, the judge believes it and the driver in the next lane believes it.

It's a self-evident truth!

But notice that self-evident truths – like I'm the boss - have exceptions - like failed resolutions, like "I forgot," or 'Well OK, I shouldn't … but just one more time.'

We trade short term gain for long term pain. A hot fudge sundae in the hand is worth more than a fat posterior in the future.

To keep our box tidy Tiny usually keeps such human but costly tradeoffs hidden in the basement of our minds.

Take a minute and think of one habit you sincerely wish your Tiny could control. Jot it down in the margin for future reference.

In the event you can't come up with one at the moment ask someone who lives outside your box to help you out. Ask someone close enough to have seen some of your behavioral garbage.

On second thought don't do that. Displaying and analyzing each other's bad habits is messy business.

Instead let's agree that from time to time Tiny has trouble controlling your behavior, let's agree that sometimes Tiny is not the boss, let's agree that occasionally Tiny simply loses it.

Chapter 3: Life Tailgates Tiny

To help Tiny regain control we need to slip outside the box and get the big picture. Recall we're using Einstein's trick, we're using *thought experiments* to help us escape and revise our habitual ways of thinking and acting.

Thought Experiment #2: Traveling the highway of life.

Think of yourself traveling on a super-highway but not at the speed of light. Notice that in order to change direction and make a safe exit you must plan ahead by gradually shifting lanes. Otherwise you're forced to go with the flow, otherwise your Tiny is not the boss.

Although this highway analogy is useful it's also *too simple*. Unlike traveling through life, highway exit signs are clearly marked, most other drivers follow the rules of the road, and with a few seconds of forward planning you have the skills and equipment readily available to effortlessly escape from the tail gating, escape from the flow and safely exit.

Navigating physical space is one thing. Navigating psychological and social space is quite another. It's much more complicated, people make up the rules of the road as they go along. Furthermore, we lack clear exit signs to guide us so we unwittingly acquire a few bad habits along the way. Then when we finally try to exit Tiny lacks the vision and muscle to navigate an escape.

Where do you get a learner's license before you start traveling on the road to boredom, fatsville, boozeburg, sweaty-palms, insomnia or divorceland?

Figure 3-1

Where do you learn to detect the early warning signs – *Exit Ahead?* Where do you learn to shift lanes soon enough to make a timely and successful escape?

Some of us learn too late, ending up at a dead end - too soon old and too late smart.

Some of us learn the hard way – we crash!

Some of us learn how to slip or slide out of our rut soon enough and long enough to get the picture and actually change direction.

Let's see how they do it.

Chapter 4: The Magic Tool

I dreamed... dreamed of escaping, "the world's great snare."

Fortunately your Tiny already possesses the tools necessary to escape from your rut - from the world's great snare. Tiny already possesses the skills of an escape artist.

For the moment forget all those failed New Years resolutions – think positive!

Thought Experiment #3: Watch your escape artist in action.

Each day Tiny automatically generates bits of freedom, automatically exits the relentless traffic of daily living.

We don't appreciate the artistry of our little escapes because we usually pull them off without thinking. Or we don't see them as opportunities - as potential first steps on a new path. Instead, we often consider our "time outs" as cop-outs.

Do any examples come to mind of the words you use to engineer exits from life's tailgating, any words you use to navigate escapes from THE RUT?

How about these?

"Just a minute, I'll be right there."

"Ok … Ok… I'll do it tomorrow."

"I couldn't do it because the damn copier (car, vacuum, computer, subway, etc.) broke down."

"I'll be late, I've got a meeting."

"Sorry, I've got a headache."

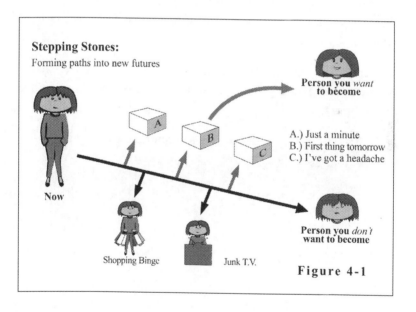

Stepping Stones:
Forming paths into new futures

Person you *want* to become

A.) Just a minute
B.) First thing tomorrow
C.) I've got a headache

Now

Shopping Binge   Junk T.V.

Person you *don't* want to become

Figure 4-1

Notice, these little exits have one thing in common - they all enable you to briefly escape the relentless flow of daily life. So the flow is not completely relentless after all. The rut isn't too deep - **yet**.

At this point, don't worry about whether your escapes are good or bad, wise or foolish - just focus on the fact that they can and do occur – celebrate the fact that Tiny can still make them happen.

So notice, if interruptions in the merciless flow can happen accidentally (at home with the flu), or unconsciously (forget an appointment), or irresponsibly (at home with a hangover), why can't they happen in a planned and positive way?

They can. And, just because resolutions and good intentions typically peter out doesn't mean they must.

All it means is that you're not capitalizing on the escape tools and skills that Tiny already possesses - as we'll see in the next chapter.

It was Cleopatra who spoke of the "world's great snare." Recall, she escaped by clutching a deadly snake - an Asp - to her lovely breast.

Fortunately, we needn't resort to such final solutions.

Chapter 5: Warning Signs

"You aughta get out more...!"

It typically requires a couple of hurtful *smacks* on your self-esteem to capture enough attention to transform your little escapes into a new path toward a better future.

In the next few chapters we'll consider examples of successful escapes. We start with Mabel who'd sold her soul an inch at a time. Fitting the stereotype of the traditional wife-mother, Mabel was locked in a box constructed of her own expectations and those of her family.

At the moment no smacks, just the old routine. Actually she did a pretty good job but her particular wife-mother box wasn't big enough any more.

In their own way her family appreciates what she does for them. However like modern families they're so busy they rarely express their appreciation, except at Christmas and birthdays. Yes she gets traditional gifts - hand lotion, chocolates, the latest food processor and can you believe it a high tech vacuum cleaner? How romantic can you get? Of course she gets cards - the kind with printed messages dripping with three dollars worth of sentimentality, underlined with the hastily scribbled X X O O.

Like many of us Mabel had gradually learned to fit into other people's expectations. Nothing wrong with that, we all have to do a lot of it to live together in the same house, work in the same setting, and drive on the same road.

But it can go too far... way too far!

As Tiny says you can sell your soul an inch at a time till there's only a small tattered corner left for you.

Mabel had pretty well given up hope that something special might happen. Given up hope that her husband or one of the kids would spring a surprise with something that showed they knew who lived inside - something special that they'd made just for her.

She rarely daydreamed anymore - dreams take her places she can't afford to go. She used to imagine that she'd take a running leap out of the rut, a leap up into something ... something ... she wasn't sure what, but it would be marvelous!

The First Smack!

It happened! Not a leap but a smack during a family argument over dinner about possible careers for their eldest daughter.

Mabel suggested nursing.

Her daughter replied scornfully: "Mum you oughta get out more - you're really out of it."

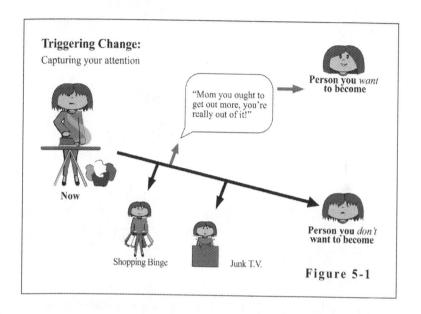

Figure 5-1

Funny how small things can lead to bigger things - modern physics tells us a butterfly flapping it's wings in Brazil may lead to a hurricane in Florida?

For the next few days as she cooked, cleaned, shopped and chauffeured, her daughter's snide comment kept echoing through her mind.: 'you aughta get out more!'"That echo, those butterfly wings, actually helped trigger some action - not a hurricane but nevertheless a little escape ... turned out to be the first solid stepping stone to "something a little bit marvelous."

Chapter 6: A Small Step into a Bigger Future

"I'm outa here… "

Mabel's daughter said it: "Mum, you oughta get out more."

That glib comment opened an old wound. Around and round in Mabel's head she heard Tiny repeating: " Mabel's boring… boring… boring."

Her husband and kids said thoughtless things – but she'd gradually become immune. However, this smack on her self-esteem made her ashamed. That shame bubbled away fuelling a resolution, not a revolt, but triggered a tiny step that eventually lead to a bigger future.

Mabel took a baby step. She resolved to get out of the house for at least an hour a day, do some window shopping and buy herself a treat – a different flavor of Tom and Jerry ice cream.

OK, so we each have our own idiosyncratic idea of sin, of living _dangerously_.

On one of her little escapes she noticed a sign in a bookstore window advertising a course in creative writing - one night a week at the local community college. She came back to that same window again the next day, and the next. Finally, she wrote down the phone number.

Tiny says; "Once you escape from your rut, even for a few minutes, you notice little paths leading off in new directions."

Even though she had the phone number Mabel didn't phone. She kept thinking: "I'm not a creative person - people would laugh… even I'm laughing."

The second smack!

When she asked her son how "e-mail" worked, he replied: "Poor old mum still back in the horse and buggy days."

That did it! Next morning she registered for the course.

Notice, it often takes a couple of smacks in quick succession to capture and hold your attention long enough to make a new move.

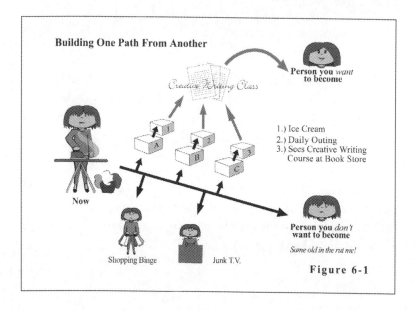

Building One Path From Another

Person you *want* to become

Creative Writing Class

1.) Ice Cream
2.) Daily Outing
3.) Sees Creative Writing Course at Book Store

Now

Person you *don't* want to become

Same old in the rut me!

Shopping Binge   Junk T.V.

Figure 6-1

Notice too that Mabel's afternoon outings consisted of a little parallel path running closely alongside her rut. But that path led to another - taking the creative writing course. She was gradually expanding and linking her islands of freedom. She was out of her rut - not permanently. She didn't want that, but out often enough to start reclaiming part of her soul.

Mabel's family didn't even notice her little *escapes.* As long as food appeared on the table and clean laundry on the shelf ... no problem. Once she developed a bit of confidence she started stretching a few of the family's expectations.

Tiny stopped whispering: "Mabel's boring, Mabel's boring," and started mumbling: "Mabel's bored, Mabel's bored."

Let's not come down too hard on her family. They were all running just to keep up with the traffic of their own lives. The fact that Mabel submissively went along with the flow is as much her "fault" as theirs. And, like most modern families, less and less time is spent at home.

That's not where the action is.

The Creative Writing Course. At the first class a bald headed guy wearing red sneakers sat down on Mable's right – he kept whispering silly asides about the lecture. On her left sat a girl with long legs and purple hair, a giggler about the age of her eldest daughter.

After class the three of them went for coffee. They agreed that their instructor smelled of booze and mints. He'd gently tease students when they read their assignments to the class: "Ah yes, echoes of Hemmingway... very distant echoes."

Their first assignment – to be read out in class – was a two-paragraph description of something they saw during the week. It should be vivid enough to make listeners feel that they'd actually been there.

Mabel admitted she was terrified of speaking in public. Purple hair added "Me too, I'll probably pee my pants." Baldy said: "Wear dark clothes, then it won't show."

On the way home Mabel realized that for the first time in ages she was having fun, furthermore people were actually listening to what she said.

By linking together a few stepping-stones into a wee path she'd taken a little leap into the mini-marvelous.

Furthermore, what her husband and kids did and said stopped being background noise. Instead Mabel started jotting bits down – grist for her first creative writing assignment.

In a few weeks Tiny said: "Hey, there's life in the ol gal yet!"

Have you got a *pet project at the back of your mind* but you've never escaped from your rut long enough to pursue it?

Chapter 7: The Future Starts Expanding

"What's got into mum?"

At first Mabel's family paid little attention. When they found out about the writing course her husband said: "Don't write anything about me" and one of her kids asked: "Will you be on T.V. like a real writer?"

As time passed her family gave her strange looks. They asked her if everything was OK - implying she might not be well. Anyway, she seemed *different*.

Surprisingly, once in a while one of them would actually sit down for a chat - mostly one sided. That was OK - that's the way kids are - full of their own stuff.

But Mabel was gradually reclaiming bits of her soul. There was somebody emerging from deep inside that she started to like. Tiny shouted "It's me... it's me... hey look we've got liftoff!"

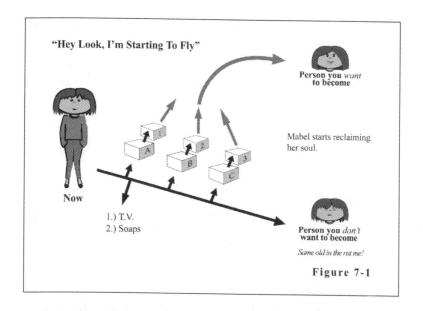

"Hey Look, I'm Starting To Fly"

Person you *want*
to become

Mabel starts reclaiming
her soul.

Now

1.) T.V.
2.) Soaps

Person you *don't*
want to become

Same old in the rut me!

Figure 7-1

Toward the end of her first creative writing course she signed up for another. She might even take enough credits to get a diploma... to graduate?

With a few misgivings she invited some of her newfound friends over one evening for a discussion group.

That event stretched some family expectations. What's happening to good ol mum? Who was this person emerging out of the kitchen, the laundry... the woodwork? She'd become ... what? They weren't sure? But she was definitely taking up more space?

How had this evolution happened, from wife/mother to *person*?

As she kept building her little paths alongside the rut, Mabel's expectations of herself started to shift from "mousy little me" to "hey, there's actually *somebody* I like inside trying to get out?"

Next, as she generated islands of freedom her ideas about her husband and kids started to change. She'd discovered that not all their expectations of her were as strong as she'd presumed - some had a long leash, some had no leash at all.

Eventually her husband finally showed signs of life: "What's this course thing you're taking all about? Who else goes?" The kids started to tease her: "Hey mom, off to see a secret admirer are ya?"

Gradually her expectations about people "out there" started to shift a bit. She found more room to play than she'd dreamed - at least dreamed in the last twenty years.

As her writing course progressed the Prof and the other students started to pay a bit of attention to what this shy housewife was writing and saying. At the last session the Prof said: "That passage Mabel just read is an excellent example of writing about what you know. She draws you in. You're there, you see it, hear it, smell it, taste it, touch it!"

He continued; "Notice you can actually inhale the fragrance of the freshly ironed clothes, you can hear the cool silence of the house in the middle of the afternoon."

The bald guy sitting next to her whispered: "Teacher's pet." The girl with the purple hair gave her a nudge.

The instructor had more to say. "Mabel's finding her voice, a sensitive, perceptive observer of her physical environment - like a delicate still-life painting. Now she's ready to move on and inject some life in her stories – some people... hopefully with flaws to make them interesting."

Everyone looked at Mabel - head down, eyes closed, beet red and hardly breathing. Till then she'd thought of her writing as "pathetic efforts"… "shitty scribbles." She never used that word out loud. But s----- scribbles or not she was actually enjoying a terrible experience.

After class, over coffee, Mabel asked for help, for suggestions about how to add flawed people to her stories. Purple hair told her to write about her family members – and their flaws. "I can't do that!" Mabel wailed, "It would be disloyal."

Purple hair shot back: "Sure you can, change the names, make things up. My mother hated me wearing hot pants so she purposely run a very not iron over the waist, the elastic deteriorated so they wouldn't stay up so I couldn't wear them."

Shaking her head Mabel said: "Oh I couldn't do that"

"You don't have to do it, all you have to do is write about it."

Red shoes chipped in his two cents worth. "Your husband sounds like a bit of a stuffed shirt, you could loosen him up by sprinkling a bit of itching powder on his colors – not really but in your story."

Mabel giggled nervously "Yes, I could change the names and they'd likely never read anything I write anyway … unless in the very improbable event that I become famous." She was obviously enjoying a terrible experience.

She was also reclaiming her soul – a bit more than an inch at a time. Whatever "got into mother" she liked it… keep it coming.

Chapter 8: Yes But ...?

"Turning Lilly pads into stepping stones. "

Have you ever tried pulling off modest escapes like Mabel's?

Julia and Sean have.

At first both failed. They tried to find stepping stones out of the rut but somehow kept slipping back in.

They'd made resolutions, Julia to build more "self- confidence", Sean to "get in better shape. "

Furthermore, they'd each successfully used their bag of tools to escape to a little island of freedom. And then ...? Well, then they didn't know what to do. Julia just sat on her bed daydreaming. She got bored and finally watched some junk T.V. Until?
Until, to her relief, someone called her back down into her rut.

Sean, actually went to the gym, built up a sweat until ... he sprained his ankle on the treadmill, and limped back down into his rut.

So, how come Mabel is doing so well, but Julia and Sean can't get started?

Answer: It doesn't take rocket science to start recreating yourself, but it does involve three musts: 1) your goal must be specific, 2) it must be affordable, and 3) you must make a "hard" commitment.

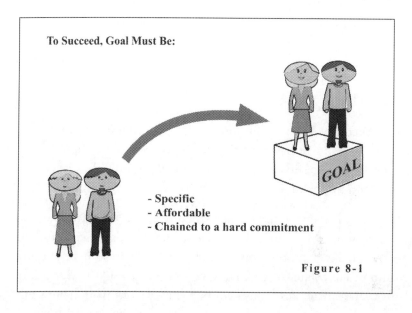

To Succeed, Goal Must Be:

- Specific
- Affordable
- Chained to a hard commitment

GOAL

Figure 8-1

First: The resolution you make – your goal – must be *specific enough, clear enough that you and other observers can determine whether you succeeded or not.*

Mabel made a specific resolution: "To complete a short-story writing course." Julia and Sean did not – they were too fuzzy, too elastic. Julia said: "To gain more self-esteem." Sean said: "To get in better shape and cut back on my boozing."

Your resolution must include not only a general goal – which both Julia's and Sean's did – but also specific courses of action and deadlines.

Mabel's resolution included both: her general goal of get out more, specifically an hour a day and buy an ice cream cone, then more specifically: "To sign up for a short-story writing course that started October 1st, for which she had to pay her fee of $50.00 by September 15th."

Which she did.

Note, that unlike Julia and Sean, Mabel included not only a specific course of action but hard deadline dates as well - deadlines beyond her control!

Second: Your resolution, your goal, doesn't have to be grandiose, but it has to be something you can start approaching now - it has to be financially and emotionally affordable. Otherwise you end up making false starts or drift into daydreaming.

Yes, I know. Some people actually do succeed turning their life around on a dime. Like? Well, like one day - cold turkey - they make a momentous change. Like giving up important things: chocolate, or cigarettes, or booze, or junk TV, or a job, or even a mate. Yes, "crash course" changes can work - but only under special circumstances - usually when you've hit bottom and there's no place left to go but up or out.

So before you hit bottom, it's smart to start with something that's not only specific, but something you can start doing immediately, with what you've got. Something you can afford - emotionally and physically - to start tomorrow – like Mabel did.

Notice, she took small steps to tiny islands of freedom toward an affordable "treat" - a new flavor of ice cream. Yes it seems trivial, but there's still a child hidden inside each of one of us. Such small rewarding steps lead to an increased sense of control helping Mabel to start reclaiming her soul a lick at a time.

Third: In addition to starting with specific courses of action and small affordable steps in order to succeed you must chain your resolution to a *clear hard commitment.*

Without a binding commitment your resolution gets shunted aside by the "normal" traffic of living. That's why New Year's resolutions fail - not only because the goal is not specific, not only because they often lack a clear, affordable course of action, but because we don't make a significant investment in the goal. To succeed you have to invest enough in the resolution so that it HURTS - personally, or publicly, or financially - if you don't give it your best shot.

As we'll see, when Sean and Julia applied these three rules - making a specific, affordable commitment they too started building alternative paths outside the rut. They too started becoming the kind of person they wanted to be.

No more trying to walk on lily pads. No more hearing Tiny whisper "plop."

Chapter 9: Making it work!

"Hey Mum look I'm walking on water... well really on the stones."

Sean and Julia can make it work if they take the last chapter to heart – if they make a hard commitment to a specific, affordable resolution.

Let's start with Sean. His goal is simpler.

Sean's Goal: "Getting in shape. "

A) *Start small, be specific*: He resolved to attend a one-hour weight-training program three times a week.

B) *Affordable:* Yes, he can afford the time and money.

C) *Hard Commitment* #1): He signs up and pays his fees at the fitness center. Hard commitment #2): He tells his Friday night beer-bull session buddies about his resolution and promises to pay for two rounds of beer whenever he skips a training session, but he can only drink one beer that night....

Notice, not only is Sean investing time and money in the course, he's making his resolution public - changing the group's expectations, triggering their vigilance - and *investing* his pride by betting on himself.

Julia's Goal: "Increasing her self-esteem." This is a classic example of a worthy but fuzzy resolution. Not only is it elastic – hard to measure – but also it depends on many factors beyond her control like the expectations and responses of others.

Julia needs a specific goal. To generate one she has to ask herself: "In what ways *specifically* am I failing to meet my own expectations?"

While on one of her islands of freedom, temporarily safe from life's tailgating, Julia realized she feels inadequate *specifically* when she's with her group of friends. She can't seem to get into the conversation? When she tries nobody pays any attention.

What can she do about it?

Notice, when you commit to a group with the same goal as yours they carry you along in the right direction – group members gain strength and direction from each other.

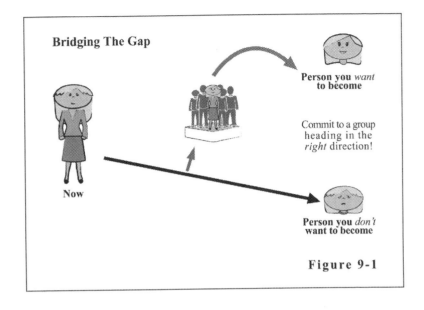

Figure 9-1

In high school Julia had been in a play and recalled that she loved it. The light went on! She started reclaiming her self-esteem by joining an amateur theatre group and ... started walking on stones.

So did Sean. By joining the weightlifting group he gained support and direction that helped carry him toward his goal. And by his public declaration and promise to his beer buddies he attracted their vigilance and friendly peer group pressure that helped keep him at it. He wasn't ready to model bathing suits just yet but the flab was slowly melting away.

Chapter 10: Trouble Shooting #1 - Breaking out and Breaking In

"When is a rut not a rut?"

Notice that up to now we've drawn the rut as a straight, solid arrow heading on a downward path into the future.

That's not accurate.

However, we needed to keep it simple to get the show on the road. Now that we've covered the basics - escape and commitment to a specific, affordable goal - we can afford to take a more realistic but still optimistic, view.

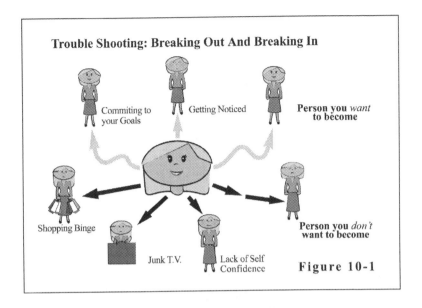

Figure 10-1

Upon magnification we see that the rut is not one straight ditch, not one solid arrow of chained behavior. Rather we find it's a zigzag of arrows, some closely and tightly welded together, others - praise the lord - only barely touching.

Weakest Link

The first rule for successful escape artists is to identify, and work on the weakest links. If you're having trouble getting enough freedom then look for and capitalize on the weak or loose links in your habit chain.

Such loose links are sometimes obvious - like when the cat's away the mice can play. Other people's expectations help keep us in the rut. When those prison *wardens* depart, or have their mind on other things, you can play - you can escape.

For example, Mabel's first escape and path-building project - window-shopping - took place in the afternoons when her mate was at work and her kids at school. Her unwitting jailers were away so she had room to play.

At first she felt nervous – but also excited - about goofing off every afternoon. Her next new path - the night class in creative writing - occurred on a weeknight when Hubby played poker with the boys, and the kids went out (scouts, football, orchestra). She didn't lie about what she was doing. She couldn't. But she didn't have to. No one even noticed.

Easy exits. Like Mabel, Julia had no trouble escaping to "do her thing" because she wasn't a highly visible figure in her group - not heavily connected within the network. That was her problem: no position, no esteem.

But even when Julia did have something interesting or important to say she had trouble breaking into the rapid flow of conversation. She had difficulty identifying a weak link - or gap in the flow through which to enter the ongoing give and take of rapid-fire talk between the popular members.

What advice would you give her?

Changing expectations. Here's what she did. She changed her own expectations. She replaced her pessimistic view of her rut as a solid arrow heading on a downward slope into a dull future. She replaced that downer with the more optimistic zigzagging, gappy chain of small arrows. She decided the first goal was not to say something interesting. Her first goal was to *get noticed!*

As indicated earlier she'd joined an amateur theatre group. At first she didn't get any speaking parts. In fact she spent most of her time painting and moving sets. Then miracle of miracles, she got her first speaking part. Only one word. Not even a word. *A SNORT!*

As the parlor maid her part called on her to give a loud snort when the leading man proclaimed he had not cheated on the leading lady.

Julia's snort started weak and small - baby steps. But under coaching her snort gradually grew, and grew, and *grew* until the director ordered her to tone it down. Her snort was upstaging the lead actors. Her snort became the topic of conversation during intermission and as patrons left the theatre after the play.

The snort traveled. You can guess what happened next. Even when off the stage her snort started to escape. It burst forth spontaneously at work, and more importantly when hanging out with her friends. When someone in her group of friends said something *dumb,* Julia's theatrical snort erupted, blasting its way into the middle of the conversation.

These explosions grabbed attention. Her friends started noticing her. "What ARE you doing?" Wisely, or shyly, she would only shake her head. Her reluctance made the group even more curious. Gradually she solved that problem too, but that's another story (hint - what topic of conversation do other's find most interesting, most captivating, most attention grabbing?)

By joining this rag tag group of wannabe actors, not only had Julia started recapturing her soul by expanding a path outside her rut, she also increased her self-esteem within the rut as well.

With group support and disclosure and commitment to his buds Sean too broke out of his rut. But now he was spending a bit too much time in front of the mirror admiring his abs.

So, the first rule of trouble shooting - whether you're trying to break out of a chain of behavior, or break into one - is to look for and work on the weakest links in the zigzagging sequence of tightly - and loosely - linked chain of behaviors of our life.

You can do it... because The Rut is not a rut after all.

Chapter 11: Trouble Shooting #2 - Goal Setting

"In order to get "there" you gotta know where "there" is.

Both Sean and Julia started out with fuzzy goals: "getting in shape" and "increasing self-esteem." But fuzzy or not they at least provided a general direction or target area to aim for.

Eventually they got their act together and aimed for and achieved specific targets.

Notice, that's what Mabel did - unwittingly. At first she just knew she wasn't the person she wanted to be, but couldn't decide who she should be. Sure, her family and other's saw her as an *OK* wife and mother. Nothing special, just *OK*.

Gradually she realized that wasn't enough. But she didn't know what *enough* would be. What would the person she wanted to be look like, feel like, act like? Her gut told her that the status quo wasn't good enough so she started escaping from the rut more frequently. By taking her time outs at the mall she started making safe little trips outa the box.

Such regular escapes, distancing her from the daily chain of events, gradually generated a different perspective, not only about her current life but also about promising and possible futures.

Don't sweat the small stuff. It may take one or two false starts before you find a compatible path. As you spend more time out of the rut you'll notice life starts slowing down - producing a kind of time-lapse view of what once appeared to be chaotic action - like the kind you see in old Charlie Chaplin films.

As you spend more time out of your rut you see your life from a *new vantage point.* You'll start noticing patterns of behavior - your own and those of important others. Now you're starting to get "the picture" and notice appealing paths into the future.

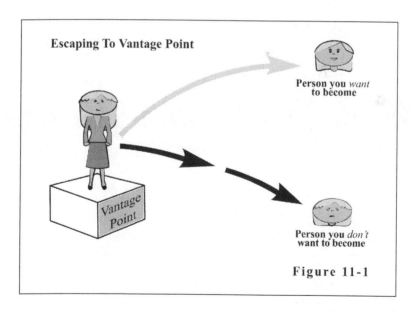

Escaping To Vantage Point

Person you *want* to become

Vantage Point

Person you *don't* want to become

Figure 11-1

Once those slow motion patterns emerge, choosing goals and setting priorities become much simpler, as it did for Mabel. Even if your new goal is small remember anything that gets you out of the rut regularly is a step in the right direction. Such escapes enable you to travel that new route with less and less effort, to gain a vantage point, to see new futures.

Then you're on your way, committing to a specific, affordable goal, building stepping stones away from the person you don't want to be toward the person you do.

If you work, it works!

Guess what? Julia starred in her own one-act play consisting of nothing but different kinds of snorts exchanged between a couple on their first date.

Tiny says: "Yes but, what if you see an appealing goal but still have trouble committing to it? "

Chapter 12: Trouble Shooting
#3: Commitment - Step 1

"I've escaped from them ... but not from me."

Even though you can pull off some escapes from the expectations of others, you may still encounter difficulty breaking free from your own expectations, your own tightly linked habits. For some reason, even though you've gained some freedom, you still can't build a new path.

Recall that initially Sean and Julia had the same problem. At first, after escaping the rut, Julia sat on her bed wondering what to do with her liberty, and Sean got bored and watched soaps ... something he never did. He was placing himself in grave danger of getting sucked into a deeper rut.

As well as possessing escape tools, you also know something about making a commitment - through investing time, money, and pride – for example through making a public disclosure of your resolution or goal. But again, even though you have that knowledge, your Tiny can't seem to make the necessary moves:

like "signing up"; "paying your fee", and publicly committing to a new course of action, even a small one.

How come? Well, you already know some of the explanations - not real answers, but culturally acceptable excuses: "You can't teach an old dog new tricks"; "old habits die hard"; etc. Intellectually, you also know some of the answers: " Every journey begins with one small step"; "This is the first day of the rest of your life - don't waste it"; "to be able to walk you must first be able to stand on your own", etc.

Yeah, yeah... but what should you do? What *specifically* should you do?

Step 1. The linkage between one piece of behavior and another is built through repetition and practice. Every time behavior A (e.g., arriving home) is followed by behavior C (e.g., turning right into the family room and flicking on the TV) the strength of the linkage between them is reinforced. So gradually you can predict: **If A then C.** Gradually behavior C becomes blindly and loyally committed to following behavior A. [1]

So, if your goal is to write the great novel, or get in shape (behavior B) then you need to gradually build a strong "**If A then B**" linkage - where B follows A like night follows day.

Let's say you already have an "If A then C" behavior link: If A (I arrive home) then C (I turn right and flick on the TV). How likely is it that the day after your Tiny decides to do some writing that you're going to arrive home (Behavior A), and instead of turning right to the family room and clicking on the TV as usual (behavior C), you're going to turn left and go to your computer and lose yourself in writing a novel or going for a run (behavior B)?

---

1 Notice behavior C can be any activity that you want to control like watching TV, smoking, drinking, hanging out, etc.

That's a big step - that hill is probably too big for Tiny's shoes.

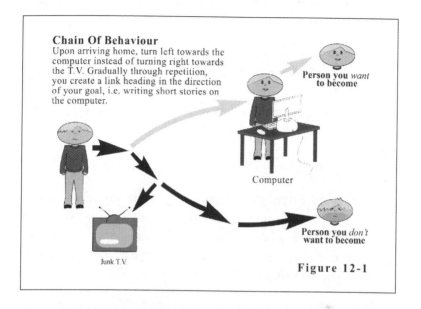

Chain Of Behaviour
Upon arriving home, turn left towards the
computer instead of turning right towards
the T.V. Gradually through repetition,
you create a link heading in the direction
of your goal, i.e. writing short stories on
the computer.

Person you *want*
to become

Computer

Person you *don't*
want to become

Junk T.V.

Figure 12-1

Capitalizing on wiggle room. Remember, there's always a little *wiggle room* - a little gap - even between two strongly linked behaviors. For example, even though behavior A (arriving home) almost always leads to behavior C (watching TV), sometimes you sneak in another behavior between the two. Sometimes, upon arriving home, you first hang up your coat (behavior X), or go to the kitchen and grab a soda and a snack (behavior Y) before you settle down to watch TV.

So? So, if you can sneak behavior X or Y in between A and C, then you can sneak in a bit of behavior B. The key word here is "bit" - even a few seconds of behavior B is enough to start establishing a new path. It's like gradually starting to wear a little rut between behavior A and B. In psychological jargon it's called "shaping."

You start building that new commitment to behavior B with baby steps. When you arrive home tomorrow instead of turning right to the family room turn left to your computer.

Gravitational pulls. When you turn left you'll feel the strong gravitational pull of the TV. Don't panic. The first time merely dash in, turn the computer on, say "hello nice computer" then sprint to the family room to catch your TV program. But remember, every time you turn left rather than right - even if the detour only lasts a minute - you're strengthening the "If A then B" linkage, and loosening the "If A then C" connection.

After several days of turning left you can afford to stretch your computer time by a minute. Now, not only do you turn on the machine and pat it, but commit - wee commitment - to typing in just one sentence - if that's too much type one word - "Title" - then rush to the TV.

But notice that after about a week of this seemingly silly behavior something magical starts to happen. You'll find yourself - effortlessly - sitting down and starting to type: maybe an e-mail to a friend, maybe a diary entry, maybe the rough idea for a short story.

What's happened?

Links to a familiar habit. Through that week or ten days of taking baby steps you've gradually linked into the chain of behavior already associated with your computer: *If D (I turn on the computer) then E (I check my e-mail). Then If E (I check my e-mail) then F (I reply to that e-mail); etc.* That simple little initial step of turning left rather than right has linked you up to one of your established behavior chains – working at your computer - a chain that's related to your new goal of writing a short story or play or novel.

By capitalizing on the gaps and wiggle room in behavior chains you can painlessly build new pathways by starting with baby steps. It works. Test it out on some task you've been avoiding or something you've always wanted to try.

Yes we know. It seems weird for a grownup to resort to infantile baby steps in order to stretch or break a habit. But remember most of our reflexes and habits work in our favor – breathing, walking, running, eating, sleeping, talking, loving, driving… without most of em we'd be dead. So there's a good reason why they're tough to break.

At this point you've reached the stage when you not only know how to temporarily escape from the expectations of others, but also how to identify and escape through gaps in your own expectations, your own behavior chains, and link up with those positive habits already going in the desired direction.

Tiny boasts: "Hey we did it, we did it. We didn't turn right to the TV once in the last three days. We just turned left to our computer… without even a pause. Then later rewarded ourselves with some TV." So the new behavior chain became: If A then B then C.

Breakthrough. A few weeks later Tiny pulled off a massive escape from marching to the drumbeat of TV scheduling. By purchasing a recording system, favorite programs could be watched when it suits Tiny's priorities, not the network schedule.

But what if taking baby steps doesn't work for you? What if your Tiny is still having trouble escaping from the flow and building a new path?

Well then you're a challenge – your Tiny needs a boost. Check out the next chapter.

Chapter 13: Troubleshooting: Commitment - Step 2

"Turning social pressure on its ear - using it to your advantage."

If you're still having trouble getting your show on the road, it's time to bring in the big guns.

Recall earlier we indicated that much of our behavior is guided by, or is often at the mercy of, strong expectations - your own and those of important others. Can you think of a way that you can turn those powerful forces to your advantage?

Here's the idea. The glue that holds civilizations, families, and friendships together consists of one thing: *shared expectations.* Think of the familiar phrases that describe the power of group pressure, of shared expectations: "I couldn't do that - what would people say?"; "I don't want to make a fool of myself."

But notice, we can use those shared expectations as driving forces to help us get to where we want to go. It's called positive *tailgating.* How do we do that? How do we capitalize on that kind of energy? Can you think of an example?

What about *giving your word?* Not only does that trigger group vigilance and pressure, but it also triggers energy deep within you because… "My word is my bond"; "I won't welsh on a bet"; "I honor a contract"; etc.

Such shared and imbedded *cultural rules* reside deep down in our guts - they're matters of pride or shame, and are reinforced by custom and law.

Strong stuff! Such emotionally-anchored personal and cultural expectations can help strengthen your resolve, can help reach your goal. If lack of commitment to that goal is keeping you in your rut it's time to access these deep reserves of power. It's time to start recapturing your soul as a matter of personal *pride and* failure to do so a matter of *shame* - a loss of face, respect.

Yes, pride and shame are strong stuff, so think carefully before taking this step.

If, after careful deliberation you decide the answer is 'yes' then read on.

Linking your new goal to powerful personal and social expectations.

You already know that there's nothing like soft, fuzzy deadlines to encourage procrastination - to justify putting things off. You also know that clear, hard deadlines usually get you off your posterior. Miss a soft deadline - so what? Miss a hard deadline and it hurts - psychologically or academically or socially or financially. So if you're still procrastinating the time has come to **chain** your resolution to rock hard deadlines.

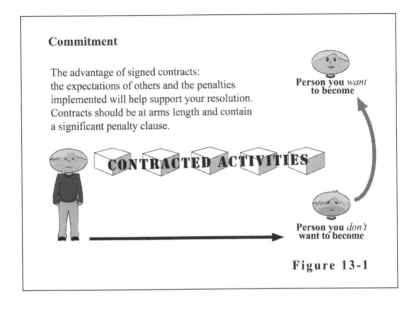

Commitment

The advantage of signed contracts: the expectations of others and the penalties implemented will help support your resolution. Contracts should be at arms length and contain a significant penalty clause.

Person you *want* to become

CONTRACTED ACTIVITIES

Person you *don't* want to become

Figure 13-1

Hard Deadlines

Hard deadlines have three things in common: You place them in other people's hands; they are clear, failing to honor them *costs you something*.

1. In other people's hands. You know that if *you* make the deadline, and only *you* know about it, you can break it anytime you choose.

How do you avoid such copouts?

By making a clear contract with someone else.

For instance, the authors of this book used a written contract to ensure that we had chapter drafts and suggested revisions back and forth to each other by specific dates. If either one failed he had to buy the other an expensive bottle of wine. The longer the infraction the more expensive the wine. We used similar contracts over the years in writing joint papers and books. It works. It not only helps you achieve your goals but also adds spice to the processes.

If you're not working on a joint project you can place the deadline and contract with an honest, hard-hearted 'judge' who monitors your progress, or lack thereof. In other words, you decide on a course of behavior (e.g., complete a 'get fit' program) then you sign a clearly worded contract, place it in the hands of an *arms length* and conscientious broker to track your performance and reject phony excuses.

You require a judge who can't be conned into letting you weasel out of your contract. Don't use a family member or a friend. They're either too softhearted or arguments may arise that threaten your relationship. Select a conscientious nerd at work, or make your contract with a lawyer. Remember at this stake you want a fierce tailgater, not a sympathetic shrink.

However, this is strong stuff so DON'T sign a witnessed contract till after you've read the final chapter of this book!

2. Clear and specific goal. In order to judge whether you have followed your promised course of action and reached your goal you must word your contract carefully. Your goal should be clear enough that both you and your 'judge' can agree whether you've met the contracted conditions or not. So, don't just sign a contract merely stating: "I'm going to complete a 'get fit' program." Rather you contract *"to sign up and pay your fees by Sept. 15, 2009, for Fitness program 101 at Seneca College, and to complete the course by December 15, 2009, attending enough classes to graduate and obtain a course certificate."*

3. Consequences. Not only do hard monitored deadlines get you up and moving in the right direction but failure to meet them must *COST YOU* something that you value: pride, money, etc. The contract should include a penalty clause agreed to by both you and your judge.

For example, if you fail to meet your contract the hundred-dollar deposit you left with the 'judge' goes to your least favored political party. Or, if you fail to meet the contract your deposit goes to buying the judge several bottles of his or her favorite wine. Notice, this makes the judge less inclined to let you off the hook if you try to weasel out – they gain if you fail.

Or, you can personalize the penalty. If you fail to honor your contract your pledge to do twenty hours volunteer work for a charity of the judge's choosing, or to wear a large sign for three hours outside your neighborhood shopping mall: the sign reads: "Don't trust me! I reneged on a signed contract." Well, maybe that's a bit much?

Use whatever penalties will force you to get you off your duff and keep you there - not just talking the talk, but walking the walk on your new pathway out of the rut.

Now you know how to turn tailgating and group pressure to your own advantage. As you repeatedly travel this new exit to your contracted activities the path deepens – it gradually become an easily traveled rut, but a rut heading in the 'right' direction.

Finally, in the last chapter we provide you with one more important trouble-shooting tool. Tiny whispers: "If you've opted for a firm contract, make sure you read the final chapter before signing it!"

Chapter 14: Troubleshooting: Commitment - Wiggle Room

"Hey... now I'm putting myself way out on a limb."

Arm's length contracts? Penalty clause? Yes, we're getting into strong stuff - particularly if you're making a major commitment of time and resources. If these hard deadlines and commitments make you feel a bit anxious they should. You need to build in some *legitimate wiggle room*.

Mediation. When making strong hard commitments you must build some flexibility into the contract. Unpredictable circumstances like illness, accidents, etc. must be considered just in case you and your appointed judge can't agree on what constitutes legitimate extenuating circumstances that warrant extensions or even cancellation of your contract.

To handle unforeseen circumstance the contract should provide for a third person - mutually acceptable to both of you and the judge - someone who mediates any contract disputes, and whose decision is final, well almost. We also recommend that you include an escape clause that allows you to void your contract in case you can't stomach or afford the contract conditions emotionally or financially.

The inclusion of a mediator and and/or a buy out clause should allay your fears. Yes? No? Still procrastinating? You're a toughie. But we have one last suggestion.

Timing. You may hear a little voice inside whispering: *"Hey kiddo, you're not just escaping from THE RUT, but you're also escaping into another kind of rut - a hard commitment, possibly with painful consequences."*

So it's normal to feel twitchy. You may find yourself putting off making such a binding commitment -*"until things settle down."*

But, you know, and we know *"things"* never really settle down.

However, you also know that your desire to make any change vacillates - sometimes weaker, sometimes stronger. That's where *timing* comes to the rescue.

When, in the normal cycle of feelings, the desire is strong - when *the iron is hot* - make your move! Pay your deposit, sign your contract - put it on the line. It's your key to a new future whereas procrastination is... well you know - it's waking up too soon old and too late smart.

Figure 14-1

P.S. But what if...?

What if you're still having trouble?

Well, if that's the case, reconsider your goal. Take some time off, put it on the back burner. Then after a breather take another crack at it.

You may find that:

1. Maybe, all things considered, you're really pretty satisfied with the person you now are - after all the rut is familiar and you've got lots of company.

2. Or, maybe you chose the wrong goal: too big? It's desirable but it's not you. So, you need more free time - out of the rut - and an appropriate goal will emerge. Recall, Mabel found her's window-shopping.

3. Or, maybe, you need an entirely different rut. Maybe you need to pack up and move. Maybe you need a rut operating with a different set of expectations - expectations supporting the kind of person you want to become. Maybe you're just slowly getting ready to make the great escape!

The more time you spend around places and people operating with different expectations the sooner you'll know if it's your preferred and compatible space. And if so you'll probably find the "lift-off energy" to pack up and move there.

But remember great escapes, such as changing careers, can also result from the smaller escapes discussed thus far. The smaller escapes gradually provide an enlarged perspective on your life, a clearer set of priorities, the strength to follow new paths.

Only you can know, only you can decide if the iron is hot, if the time is ripe for a big breakout, a big breakthrough.

But before making that kind of radical change in lifestyle we strongly recommend that you consult a professional counselor.

By the way, you look different... somehow better ... have you done something with your hair ... or maybe your point of view?

GOOD LUCK!

Appendix

Workbook Checklist

1. **Goals:**
   a) **General:** _____

   _____

   _____

   _____

   _____

   b) **Specific:** _____

   _____

   _____

   _____

   _____

2. **Hard deadline(s):** _____

   _____

   _____

   _____

3. **Affordability:**
   a) Time: _____
      _____
      _____
      _____

   b) Money: _____
      _____

   c) **Significant other support (who will support & who will block change?)**
      Supporters: _____
      _____
      _____
      _____

      Blockers/foot _____
      draggers: _____
      _____
      _____

4. **Contract terms:**
   a) Goal(s) _____
      (specific): _____
      _____
      _____
      _____

   b) **When? (Date & time):**
      Start: _____
      _____

End: _____

_____

c): Penalty _____

_____

_____

d) Judge? _____

_____

e) Escape clause: _____

_____

f) Mediator: _____

_____

Notes